MINDFUL KIDS

A complete Guide to Help your Child Focus and
Succeed in School and Life

Written By
Susan Garcia

1

medical or professional advice. The content within this book has been derived from various sources. Please consult a licensed professional before attempting any techniques outlined in this book.

By reading this document, the reader agrees that under no circumstances is the author responsible for any losses, direct or indirect, which are incurred as a result of the use of information contained within this document, including, but not limited to, — errors, omissions, or inaccuracies.

Contents

Chapter 1: Introduction

Any important life skills—concentration is one of them—is best taught when the person is still young. There is a saying, "Shape the steel while it's hot," which suggests that the parents should take action and help shape the kid's future while they still can.

If one is to wait too long, bad habits will form and be reinforced, making it hard to pick up good habits and drop bad ones. Jordan B. Peterson also mentioned in one of his talks that parents should encourage good behaviors in children. They should be able to play by themselves even at the rough-and-tumble play. A good indicator for the parents that they have helped shape the child's future (at least, socially) is when all the other kids want to play with them at the age of four.

Similarly, parents should encourage other behaviors to help children succeed academically. Therefore, concentration is important.

Concentration is like a muscle. In order to strengthen it, regular exercise is required. Some kids are lucky because they are born with a better concentration, but that doesn't mean it cannot be changed. All kids can learn and practice many things to help them. That way, their ability to focus and maintain their attention improve.

Being able to concentrate for a long time is important in school. When kids get older, they also have more activities after school that require even more concentration. It goes without saying that kids can concentrate on activities that are fun or enjoyable. Unfortunately, almost every single activity in school is not even slightly enjoyable. That will bore them very quickly and make them lose focus.

To be fair, it is boring for everyone, even for adults, unless it's from a favorite class.

Anyone would rather play video games or go out rather than sit and listen for hours at a time. Still, the ability to focus regardless of how boring the task is very important because it helps the kids learn and improve, leading to self-confidence and positive self-esteem.

Concentration is very similar to mindfulness, which is a concept that receives a bit of attention in popular culture when it was discovered that mindfulness practices (such as meditation, or deep breathing) can serve as effective forms of stress-relief.

Mindfulness is the ability to focus on one thing at the moment. It is not one of those scams on the internet, either. Mindfulness is shown to have many mental health benefits, including increased happiness, stress management, and most importantly, improved academic and test performance. Mindfulness requires focus – concentration.

However, the ability to concentrate alone is not

enough. There are several other skills that kids need to learn, one of which is being able to communicate properly. This is, again, explained by Jordan Peterson. When a child is able to communicate properly, they will be able to become a better person when they grow up. Those who fail to learn communication skills will grow up to be at least awkward, and will have a hard time adjusting to new environments.

Some children may also have a hard time eating. It should be clear that, if a child does not eat enough, there will be problems. Their development will be ruined, making it hard for them to do some jobs, both physical and mental ones. They will also fall ill easily, making life harder for them to enjoy.

Therefore, this book will talk about the three main things that children need to do if they want to succeed in life: concentration, socialization, appetite. Though it may seem easy, each of these elements has several different points of their own.

This book serves as a guide for both children and their parents to understand how to overcome some challenges of raising a child. Children too can follow along with the guides in this book and perhaps even discuss some of the tips in this book with their parents so they can create a routine that benefits both the child and parents. Parents would know exactly what their children want to make them happy.

Chapter 2: How to Be Focused

Parents often tell their children to stop fidgeting and finish their homework. It is difficult for kids to remain focused on any work without getting too distracted. It is not their fault when you think about it. Children are naturally energetic, and so parents should not expect their children to remain focused completely for hours at a time, and not getting distracted. Still, it is possible to help a child focus on a task and increase concentration skills for a longer period of time.

It is important to point out that children are different than adults. When they are given a task that isn't fun, they get bored and their focus change to something more interesting. Then again, many adults are also easily distracted as well. Thankfully, there are ways to improve concentration in kids. These tips are designed with the understanding of the children's mind so they can prove to be very effective.

Focus Games and Exercises

Because children focus more on fun activities, it is best to try and make their activities a little more fun. Whatever it is, make sure to keep gadgets, tablets, and computers away. Children should instead play with normal toys or do activities that improve their attention, and concentration exercises. Now, some may ask why the use of gadgets, tablets, or computers are not allowed. That is a good question. Many scientific studies have shown that they actually reduce the attention span and memory power in children. Therefore, they should be used sparingly or not at all.

Thinking Games

Children's ability to concentrate and focus can be improved by letting them play concentration games that require thinking, use of memory, and planning. There are plenty of crossword puzzles, jigsaw puzzles, as well as card games that do just that. Games like "Memory" or "Uno" help improve attention for words, numbers, as well as pictures. When it comes to puzzles, something as simple as "Find the Difference" between two pictures or games that require them to look for a certain thing in a pile of other things also help them improve attention and increase concentration.

Sequencing

There is a strong link between sequencing and concentration. Things such as following recipes, setting the tables or putting things in alphabetical order help kids who have concentration difficulties.

Sit

Consider this a challenge. This game involves challenging the kids to sit in a chair without moving or fidgeting and see how long they can do it. Another fun game for kids is called "Statue!" which also helps improve their concentration.

In this game, the parents should play as the Curator, who stands at the opposite end of a field while the children stand at the other end. Here, the children play as the Statues, and they need to race across the field to tag the Curator. However, whenever the Curator turns around to face the Statues, they must freeze in their position and hold the pose as long as the Curator looks at them. Though the Curator can get close and investigate (or taunt) the Statues, he or she must be careful because if their back is turned to any Statues, then they can move toward the Curator. However, if a Statue is caught to be moving while the Curator looks at it, then the Statue need to return to the starting line or be eliminated.

Here, the objective of the game is for the Statues to sneak up to the Curator while his or her back is turned, without getting caught running. The first Statue to tag the Curator becomes the new Curator. The game can be repeated as many times as possible.

Though the game is fun mainly on the Statues' side, the Curator can spice everything up getting the Statues to laugh or even smile. That is enough to send the Statue back to the starting line. Overall, this game is great for children.

Environment

Some children are able to focus when they are in an environment that is soothing and calming. Some do better in the hustle and bustle environment. Knowing the best environment allow both the parents and children to design a working environment that helps children focus.

Ambiance

Start with the sound. Using soft instrumental music as well as soft lighting helps set the mood for studying. As mentioned earlier, some kids do better in a bustling environment. If that is the case, then create the same environment using such an ambiance. YouTube should have plenty of music and sounds to help children study. Speaking of using gadgets...

Gadgets

Normally, all gadgets such as iPads, smartphones, or televisions should be switched off or kept in a different room to prevent distractions. However, if studying involves the use of a computer, then try to make it so that the children can only use it for studying and nothing else. Many devices also offer parental controls that help restrict what children can do on the computer.

Materials

Arrange the workspace in a way that the children can reach everything. That way, they don't have to get up to reach anything, which would distract them. Things such as homework books, crayons, textbooks, pencils, or even water should be kept on the table or close by. This also helps children keep track of their work and help them manage their time better, which lead to increased focus and attention.

Food

How a child concentrates has a link to eating healthy food. There are many different foods that help improve children's attention. Junk food or sugary food all make children sluggish. On the other hand, food rich in proteins like almonds, eggs, and lean meat can all improve awareness and concentration levels in children.

Caffeine

A recent study found that, in the United States, children are starting to drink more and more coffee or caffeinated energy drinks, which give them a lot of sugar. While it helps to give them energy, it will lead to more tiredness later. So, avoid drinking those if possible.

Green Food

A study in the United Kingdom shows that baked beans or toast for breakfast improve the function in children's minds. Many experts say that greens or fruits also give the body substances that boost brain power.

Routines

It is important to have a schedule for children, but it can still be flexible. Here's an example:

The child returns from school at 3.30pm, have some snacks and then go out at four to cycle or play with other children. Then, at 5, the child comes back home, wash up and have some more snack before studying at 5.30. This study session lasts for 2 hours until 7.30 which is dinner time. Finally, bedtime is at 8.30.

This is a very strict schedule, but it works for some people. Again, it does not need to be this strict and should be flexible. This helps with time management and helps program the mind of children to know when they have to study or sleep. Children will eventually develop a habit of doing a certain thing at a certain time. That way, there won't be a time when children have to argue with their parents when it is time to sleep.

Naps and Breaks

Many children can concentrate better when they have enough sleep. This goes hand-in-hand with the previous point because going to sleep and waking up at specific times improve the overall quality of sleep.

A power nap that lasts for twenty minutes after school or in the afternoon also helps improve concentration in children. Just remember that any naps that last longer than twenty seconds can actually be bad because that twenty-minute nap is intended to improve focus while the shorter or longer period of napping does not do that.

Breaks should also be timed properly if possible. Bathroom breaks, hunger, and other things that require a short break should be taken care of before study time begins because those breaks often disrupt concentration.

Cut 'Em Up

Every parent should not expect children to be able to study an entire chapter in one go. It is possible but very difficult for a child. It helps to break all tasks down into smaller ones. In this case, the chapter should be divided into pages or even paragraphs so the child can feel that they have completed something, which will make them want to do more. This is also the same for household chores as well.

It is also worth trying to set a time limit for any goal. If it is studying, then try to set a goal to read through a number of pages within 20 minutes. Do remember that the average time for an adult to concentrate is about 42 minutes, and so the time can be a lot shorter for children. Therefore, it is a good idea to set up a shorter time period for children such as fifteen minutes or twenty minutes.

Moreover, some children do better when their goals have a time limit. Others, however, might feel pressured, feeling anxious, and begin to lose focus.

Method of Learning

Every single child learns differently. Some take in lessons easier when they see it. Some do it better by hearing, while some study when they know about it and can touch it. Some do better when they have all three.

It is important to know which category the child falls under because then their study can be designed to suit them better. This means the child can understand and remember better. So, how to tell if a child studies by seeing, hearing, or touching?

Learning by Sound

Here, children do best from traditional teaching techniques. Many teachers use these techniques by talking to their students and explaining the lessons. Another thing that helps these kids maintain focus and interest is the use of voice tone or body language. Children who learn by sound do better when the directions are read aloud when they need to talk, and basically, everything is done through talking.

Learning by Sight

Other students depend on visuals – seeing the lessons. It can be summed up into a short phrase, "Show me, and I will understand," These children learn better when diagrams, charts, pictures, films, and written directions are used. They will also perform better when they have a to-do list to complete, assignment logs to follow as well as written notes to help them understand the lesson. This method of teaching is often shown in science class in which the teacher shows the students how some chemical reaction works, which often does wonders in getting the children to remember the lesson. Many techniques here are also helpful for children who learn by touch.

Learning by Touch

Many children are successful when they learn through touch. That means feeling, experiencing, or simply playing with the material at hand. This is probably because learning this way is the closest thing to playing with a toy at school, which is both exciting and useful. Many children start off learning through touch by moving and touching everything when they learn. Around second or third grade, some can learn by simply seeing the idea. At the late elementary years, some more students, especially females, can learn through listening. Still, many adults, especially males, often benefit from learning by doing. This type of learner do best when they are engaged with the learning activity. They learn the fastest when they perform experiments in a science lab, field trip, dance, or other activities.

Designing the Study Method

When the best learning method of children is found, it is time to design the study method that they can follow which suits them the best.

For children who learn by sight, start by using flashcards. If they are learning spellings or ideas, write them down on small cards and show them repeatedly to help them understand and learn faster. Asking them to draw what they are studying also helps them as well because they need to think of an image that shows what they have learned. This involves the use of sight, which is linked to their method of learning as well. Another plus here is that asking them to draw help develop their fine motor skills. Doodling also helps because it helps children recall what they have been studying at that point and remember it at a later time.

For children who learn by sound, reading the lesson aloud or listening to someone else reading it is enough. Audiobooks work better than paper books in this case.

For children who learn by touch, practicing the ideas in the lesson is the best way for them to learn. For example, if the child needs to learn the solar system, then why not create an activity for it? Here, one of the ways involves creating a model of the solar system itself and color it.

Prepare for the Next Task

When the children are busy, allow for a few minutes for them to stop and start a new activity. Here, it helps because when the children are focused on one task, it can be hard for them to stop doing it and start something else, especially if it is something that they love to do.

Reward

Having a reward system encourages children to focus as well. They don't have to be tokens like chocolates or toys. They can be praises or even more studying. For example, some children study better when they have gummy bears once every ten pages in the book that they read. Others love to solve math problems but hate studying English. So, the best way to reward them when they study English is by letting them study math as a reward for studying English.

Distractions

Because children are normally energetic, allow them some time to vent out the extra energy when they have completed a task. It can actually help them focus better on the next task because their needs for entertainment is completed for a time, and so they can return to studying. It helps if the child gets to do something different during this short break. For example, letting the child play with some toys after a few spelling lessons.

Energy

Again, all children are different. Some are full of energy in the morning while some are in the evenings. So, it is a good idea to cater the schedule to fit this preference, so to improve focus. During the high-energy times, start by doing tougher activities. When the energy level goes down, change to lighter activity.

Meditation

There are many relaxation techniques out there. Some involve the use of deep breathing, whereas others use positive images to help the brain to improve or learn new things. Combining these techniques help children a lot. This helps create a certain behavior. For example, ask the children to close their eyes and picture themselves in a class, studying. Ask them what can they see, hear, or feel. Ask them to find out what is distracting them and how they would take care of those problems. When done, their behaviors at school should also be changed.

Chapter 3: How to Reduce Screen Time

Everyone has listened to the radio and ended up singing all day long. People have seen a scary movie or a short scary clip that keeps them awake at night. It is normal to cry along with the characters in that TV series.

This just shows that the impact of screens is huge in people's lives. It is so much so that what people hear and see change the way they think. This applies to adults, but children are easier to be influenced. That means, what children see and hear will shape them as a person for the rest of their lives. Therefore, it is important to make sure that only the good things come in in order for children to develop into a good and competent person. The internet itself is huge, with millions of useful contents that children can learn from. At the same time, however, there is also equally plentiful harmful content out there.

In today's digital world, one needs to ask whether or not is it ideal for children to be completely cut off from their screens? After all, because parents need to work longer hours, they often use gadgets and smart screens or other devices to keep their children occupied. So far, these devices give children creative and engaging content for the young mind.

It is worth pointing out that screen time is a problem for parents because children nowadays are digital children. Nowadays, it is impossible to separate children completely from technology because that will just mess with them in the future. At the same time, they should use those devices only to study, which is often not the case. Therefore, achieving a balance is needed.

The Line

As a start, both parents and children need to know what screen addiction is. It is when someone has been staring at a screen and using a device for so long that they end up feeling that they can get all the entertainment they need from the device. This can easily reach a point where people want to stare at their smartphone whenever they have the chance. The screen is just as deadly, if not deadlier, than illegal drugs. It can easily ruin a child's future. But how does such a device can do such a thing?

From here, things can be a bit difficult to understand, but try to keep up. Basically, the screen triggers the reward part of the brain, which makes the child feels good, as if they have done something great. Feeling such a way is fine because people feel that way after they completed a hard job, which pushes them to do better tasks. This feeling is addictive, which is why some people keep doing great things. However, when the screen can provide with the same feeling, one can be hooked to it very easily. At the same time, it is just as dangerous for children because it can ruin their development. So, what happens if a child has a screen addiction?

Problems with the Body

Nowadays, many children have neck pain, which is a common problem that adults face over the last decade. Now, children have it too. Why is that? Posture.

Many children lie down, slouching over, or sitting down and bending over just to look at their smartphones. Doing so causes their backbone to change. This change affects the blood flow throughout their body, especially to their brain, slowing down their development. Too much screen time has the following problem to the child's body:

Headaches

Not many people know that the screen produces blue light. That is why there is an orange or yellow light app to help ease the eyes. Stare at a screen with blue light for too long and children will be bound to have a headache. The problem is that when a child has a headache, many times, they cannot focus, let alone do anything properly. This is very understandable. Even adults do not want to work when they have a throbbing headache. That means, too much screen time affects a child's performance both at school and at home.

Poor Vision

This should be obvious from the start. Many children nowadays wear glasses more than the last generation. This is also caused by staring at bright blue light for too long, even for adults. With bad vision and headaches, children will have a hard time participating in sports or other activities.

Reduced Physical Activities

Just last decade, most children play outside to entertain themselves. Nowadays, many children don't do that as often anymore. Why should they go play outside when they have their tablet with them that they can use to watch millions of videos online? They can have just as much fun, if not more fun, watching these videos or playing video games. They are right, in a way. To them, physical activity will seem more like a chore than a fun thing to do.

Still, if they don't go out and play as often, the muscles

and body will become weak because they did not get as much fresh air, sunlight, etc. All of these are very important for a child's development. Plus, as mentioned earlier, children whom others want to play with at the age of 4 is well on their way to becoming socially successful adults.

Physical activities give children a great opportunity to make new friends, learn important life skills, communicate, practice teamwork, and many more. Without physical activity, the child's ability to socialize is also affected, which could lead them to become introverted or having no friends. No parent wants that to happen to their child, and no children want to have no friends either.

Posture

Another obvious side effect of too much screen time is that it affects how children stand, sit, etc. When a child, or even an adult, stare at a screen for too long, they tend to bend over without even noticing it. This forces them to keep themselves in an unhealthy position for a long time, causing neck pain, lower back pain, etc. How?

There is an image going around Facebook showing people shaped like an "f" to show how addicted to social media. This is not just a joke. When people use their devices for too long, this is how they normally end up sitting for both adults and children. Television is not safe, either. Children often sit and watch TV with their head tilted to one side, which also leads to neck pain and posture problems.

Obesity

1 out of 3 children in America is obese, according to the American Heart Association. Obesity is a serious health problem that is directly linked to too much screen time. This is because they spend their time inside their homes, watching videos or playing games instead of going outside and doing physical exercises or activities. They can easily become couch potatoes, and fatten up very quickly. In the future, they will run into other health problems such as heart problems or high blood pressure, which are very bad.

Sleep Cycle

Too much screen time is also shown to disrupt sleep. When a child, or even an adult, spend too much time watching TV or other devices before bedtime, the result is a hard time sleeping. This is because staring at a blue light makes the brain think it is still daytime, so it keeps the body active, even if it is 2 in the morning. That is why people who cannot sleep are told to not stare at their screen at least half an hour before bedtime. It allows the body to change into the resting mode, resulting in better sleep. Without proper sleep, anyone would feel groggy in the morning, which affects their daily routine and their health.

Problems with the Mind

Some children will become angry when their parents take away their devices. That is because they can no longer get the fun things out of their phones or tablet. When something, let's say a video, is entertaining to the children, that video will reappear in the child's mind again and again for a long time. This leads to their creativity being reduced.

Another problem is that children between 5 and 12 especially, learn from their surroundings. They develop their language skills, social skills, interpersonal skills, confidence, communications skills, by looking at others, especially their parents. When a child spends a lot of time on their tablet, they don't have the time or opportunity to talk to others and develop as a person. There are also other problems.

Imagination

As mentioned earlier, a child's creativity and

imagination will be reduced when they have too much screen time. Those two are important to a child's development. Before, children only needed a cardboard box to play. Building a couch fort is perhaps one of the best things ever for children. From an adult's view, it is just a cardboard box or a couch. But for children, they can see a magnificent and powerful castle, and that they are its ruler. When was the last time it happened? Well, the answer is right in front of them, if they are holding their smartphones or tablet right now.

All of their imagination is being shown to them in those devices, and the images in them are in the mind of children for a very long time. As a result, they do not have a lot of time to think on their own and become creative and imaginative.

Losses

Video games make life simpler for children, at least their lives in the game anyway. When they have to do something hard in the game and lose or get something bad, they can always restart. Many games have a saving system, which allows players to jump back in time to that moment when they saved and start again from there. Almost every single game also have a difficulty setting, which allows the player to change how hard the game will be. This allows children to avoid the disappointment of losing.

While this may seem good on the surface, it is actually very bad. Everyone should learn to accept losses and that bad things are a part of life. When children have too much screen time, they will be unable to withstand losses in real life, which makes them feel frustrated.

Moreover, there is this thing called instant gratification, which basically means getting the good stuff right now even if it means not getting more of them later on. Video games or smartphones give children the fun that they want right now. All they need is to just press a few buttons here and there, and they are given all the fun they wanted immediately. That, again, does not seem bad. But when one looks deeper, the problem can be seen.

Just like the ability to accept losses, children won't be able to learn a few virtues in life such as practicing patience or giving up the good now in order to get something even better in the future. They will develop a habit of wanting everything right now. This impatience will not get them very far in life.

Anxiety and Depression

It should be obvious from the start, but children are easier to become depressed or anxious when adults take away their devices. Most of the time, children will argue and try to stay on the screen for as long as possible. Even if the adults managed to get their child off-screen, they would not be interested in talking to their friends, which means they cannot practice their communication skills.

Violence

It is true that video games are not directly linked to violence in adults, but they can be for a child. It is stated many times already that children will learn from everyone and everything that happens around them. They will then try to do what they see.

For example, if a kid plays a lot of action games, they will see a lot of shooting, hitting, punching, etc. They will be exposed to some level of violence, and they will often try to imitate those in terms of being more aggressive. Unfortunately, they do not become violent knowingly. They might be rude, and often picks fights with their siblings, classmates, or friends, without knowing that they are more violent than usual.

Social Interaction

The worst effect of television or devices for children is that they become disconnected from society. Many research has shown that children who spend too much time on television or smartphones will be less sociable. That means, they will spend a lot less time with their friends, and in the future, they will be an antisocial person, and they will have a hard time in life. Why is that?

Communication is one of the most important parts of a child's development. With more screen times comes fewer communication times. Without communication, they will not really know what is right and wrong because they often have not been told that they are wrong from their friends. Their opinions will become biased, and they will not know how to interact with other people.

Other Problems:

With all the previous points discussed, it becomes clear that too much screen time could lead to a child's development, making it hard for them to create and maintain relationships with their friends. It is okay for children to be curious about technology and play around for a bit, but when they become too involved, they will often have a hard time understanding the real world in terms of touch, smell, etc.

Solution

Thankfully, there are a few things that both children and their parents can do in order to minimize screen time.

Boredom

Whenever a child is feeling bored, most parents would whip out their smartphone and let their children play the games in it. Why? Because they feel that they are responsible for saving their kids from boredom, and the quickest solution (though not the best) is their phones. That is not recommended, and boredom is not all that bad. In fact, it is an opportunity to get creative.

Instead of using a smartphone to pass the time, why not think of other activities to do so without involving a screen?

Other Activities

Slowly shifting children from using the screen to other activities that involve creativity is the best way to go. Start off by finding out what the kid likes. Do they like drawing? Singing? Dancing? Cooking? Knowing their interests helps because it can be used to change their habit from looking at a screen into doing something a lot more creative.

In fact, this technique could be used to develop hobbies for children. Sometimes, a child's hobby may involve classes. For example, if they like playing the piano or guitar, then arranging to have a piano or guitar lesson is the way to go.

Sometimes, kids are more interested in nature. So, try to encourage them into planting like sowing seeds, watering plants, or going for a walk among nature. It will work wonders on them.

Other Ideas

Here is something children can do instead of looking at the screen:

Hobbies

As stated earlier, engaging children in other activities are a good way of getting them into a hobby. It helps take the child away from the screen. Hobbies include paintings, puzzles, drawing, dancing, etc. If possible, the child's parents should also participate as well so to make the child become interested immediately. If the kid likes reading, then give them a new book once a week and reward them for completing each book. Rewards help keep the children interested in their hobbies, which means more time being away from the screen.

Sports

It is true that not every child wants to play sports. However, there is always some form of active play that they are interested in. Those activities in the field will surely get them and their mind away from the screen. It is the best way to go because there are many benefits in addition to being away from the screen. They can still have fun, but they will also get to build their motor skills, strengthen their bones and muscles, and improve their immune system.

There are also other activities that do not require going outside, in case it rains or something. Games like chess help improve their cognitive skills, coordination skills, as well as decision-making skills, among many others.

Chores

This can be a bit hard to do because no one likes doing chores, even adults. So, having a reward system set up is helpful in this case. It takes the child away from the screen and allows some more bonding time between parents and their children. It also teaches children about cleanliness, discipline, time management, and how to look after themselves.

Time

Sometimes, children will have a specific time when they look at the screen. This habit needs to be dropped. Breaking a habit can be hard, but there are a few fun ways to do it. For example, it is a good idea for parents to sing along with their children to a song after picking them up from school if they usually look at their phone when they are on the way home. Try to find that time when children look at their phone and come up with a different activity to get them away from the screen. Perhaps taking the child outside for a walk among nature, or taking them to a class they like, or anywhere outdoors.

If that is difficult, then it is also possible to allow for some screen time. That can tie in with the current habit for children. It is hard to drop a habit, but it is possible to at least stop it from becoming too bad. Instead of turning off the television completely, allow for some time for children to watch. For example, they can only watch one or two shows during the day. Nothing more, nothing less. They can use a mobile phone, play on their PlayStation, or watch TV, but they need to stop after, say, an hour or so.

Moreover, children should get to decide when they can get their screen time. If parents just force a schedule onto them, it just won't work because children will not follow it. However, if both parents and children agree on a schedule, well, everybody wins. If children have to use a computer or mobile phone to complete some school assignment, have a time limit. Other than that, make sure that they know how much time they have left once in a while so they can get off easier.

From there, try to introduce them to slow changes. It isn't right to ban children from watching TV or playing games on smartphones immediately. Slow changes are better so children can slowly adjust. A good start is by cutting down an hour of screen time a week.

Along the way, introduce new activities, which have been discussed earlier. Moreover, if children get their screen time because it is their favorite show in TV or a new game, allow them about an hour or so of screen time a day, but make sure they go out and play. Getting up, eating, stretching, and playing outdoors all help children develop, after all. Getting children into this habit is important.

Support

Sometimes, the children cannot be blamed when they watch TV or play with smartphones. After all, many adults do just the same. It isn't right to blame them just because they do the same thing. Instead, offer support. Children always try to do what the adults around them do. Therefore, it falls under the adult's responsibility to offer support by communicating. So, it is best to set some time in the day and talk to each other, parents and children, to strengthen the bond. What a child needs in their early age is love and support. Without these two, they cannot grow up into a good person.

For instance, just set aside about 2 hours a day during which every family member put their devices away and go do something fun together. Use the time to play, go out, and spend time together. If the weather is foul, just stay in and play some family games. There are plenty of them, and everyone will get to bond and have fun together.

It is clear that family time is one of the strongest cures

against screen addiction. Actions that seem simple (and even boring) like family dinner, going for walks, quick trips and picnics, give a chance for the family to talk to each other. This is a great opportunity for both parents and children to get to know each other better. Now, it is true that a family member understands each other the best, but it doesn't happen on its own. It is a result of constant communication among family members, which strengthen the bonds and trust between each other. For a child, this is very important because they will know that they have someone to rely on.

Without it, a child will look for other ways to fulfill their needs for a companion. That means smartphones, etc.

Gadgets

At some point, children will feel tempted to ask their parents for a smartphone because all their friends have one. It is at this point that many parents will often listen to their children and buy one, but that will only increase screen time. Both parents and children should know that those gadgets should only be used for utility, meaning using it to complete a task, not for entertainment. If a computer or smartphone is needed to complete school work, then children should only use it just to complete school work, and parents should also monitor the activity of their children, just in case something goes wrong. Of course, the use of gadgets is not all that bad. Sometimes, a phone could be a lifesaver when the child gets lost or something. In that case, a simple phone will be enough.

Chapter 4: The Importance of the Diet

Many people understand the importance of a good, balanced diet to the development and growth of a child. However, not many people know or understand the importance of creating healthy eating habits and teaching children to appreciate healthy and different food at an early age.

Here, the key is to get that balance between exposing children to different foods and the right amount to keep them healthy. The food they should eat should be high on starch such as grains or their flours like homemade French fries, baked potatoes, pasta, bread, or rice. These foods are a good source of energy for the kids and often contain vitamin B.

Moreover, children's diet should also have fruit and veggies, in several daily servings. They are low in calories or protein, but they pack a lot of vitamins and minerals which are very important for their health and growth. Different protein-rich foods such as chicken, meat, fish, or lentils are also important to help them grow stronger muscles or repair their body.

Dairy products such as whole milk, cheese, as well as yogurt are also great sources of protein, vitamins, minerals, and calories.

Real Food

The best way to describe it is by keeping everything simple and eat whole foods in their most natural state. Also, appreciate their yummy goodness. It goes without saying that fresh is best. That means, processed food must be avoided at all costs. Sometimes, children may be encouraged to eat something when they learn an interesting fact about it. So, why not tell them about the cow that produces the milk that they are drinking? Try to make that almond milk at home, or explain the difference between whole food and the thing they from a box. Try to make the food "fun" to eat, make them interested.

Plant

Sometimes, children appreciate eating the food that they have to work for – not in the sense of hard-work under the hot sun, but in a way that makes them understand where their food comes from. Just like the previous point, the idea is to make children interested in healthy foods. So, try to let them plant a few things in the backyard or in a vase near the window and let them take care of the crop. They will appreciate food even more and are more than willing to eat healthy food because they understand what it means to grow one.

Shopping

Of course, going shopping with children can be difficult for the parents. However, there are a lot of things to be gained from going shopping with them once in a while. For a start, a quick trip to the store or farmers market can teach children the fact that food does not magically appear on the shelves. Here, the seasons of the food can also be taught, and the lessons of where food comes from could be explained. It is also possible to engage the kids in shopping and make the whole activity fun such as letting them pick out a piece of produce from each color of the rainbow or choose a new ingredient they want to try out in the food they eat.

Cooking

Getting children into cooking is also a great and fun way to get them into appreciating the food that they eat.

Cooking a meal from scratch is rewarding in itself, but many parents forget that. Moreover, cooking with children serve as a way of bonding as well, not to mention that it helps children practice concentration because they follow recipes.

Unfortunately, many families nowadays have ignored the potential in cooking. They have lost touch with their kitchens and ovens serve as cabinets. Many meals now come straight out of a box or a take-out container instead of stoves. Cooking for the family is a great way to control what everyone eats because you get to choose which ingredients go into the pot.

Besides, cooking is a great way for parents to spend time with their kids, not to mention that the young ones will also learn about ingredients and flavors as well as experimentation with new foods. Children are actually more willing to try out new food if they helped cook it. Another obvious benefit is that the child also learns how to cook, which is always a useful skill to learn when they eventually move out. At least the parents need not worry that they will only have McDonald's hamburgers or pizza from Pizza Hut when they can cook and eat healthy meals.

Taste

It should go without saying that parents should eat with their kids. They should enjoy the same food together because it is a form of bonding and a way of showing love and affection which the children will need during the early stage of their life. Many people eat the food that they enjoy but hardly savor the taste. Worse yet, they take their food for granted. Everyone should take the time to taste, not just eat, and children should be taught to do the same, so they will appreciate what's on their plate more.

Talk and Teach

A third of the US children are overweight, according to the data from the U.S. Centers for Disease Control and Prevention. Nowadays, people live in a society dominated by processed food companies that control the grocery stores and markets. It is important for children to know where their food comes from, how it is grown, and how it helps their body in terms of health and functions. Many people have stopped eating for the substance inside. Instead, they eat for pleasure, or for the sake of it. As long as it tastes good, then many people would eat it, regardless of what is contained inside or whether it is healthy or not. Therefore, children need to learn how to love fruits and veggies as much as chicken nuggets, not because of how they taste (although it helps to cook them to make them taste good), but because of how it makes the body feel fresh and good. Understanding the difference in the body when it digests unhealthy food versus healthy food is crucial to get the point across.

Labels

Children need to have a basic understanding of the food that they eat. Most of the time, all the information they need will be on the label of the food package under the big "Nutrition Facts."

Start with understanding the serving information at the top. This shows the size of a single serving as well as the total number of serving for that package.

Then, check the total calories per serving. Be careful about the number of calories per serving, especially if children eat the entire package because they will be eating several servings. It is important for children to understand that, if they eat the entire package, they will take in all of those calories, which is not so good.

Children also need to know the limit of intake for total fat, saturated fat, cholesterol, sodium, etc. The amount depends on the age, gender, as well as activity level. Many government health agencies recommend limiting these.

Next on the list is understanding which nutrients are needed every day, such as fiber, protein, calcium, vitamins, iron, and other nutrients.

Finally, they need to review percent Daily Value that shows the percentage of each nutrient in a single serving. The daily recommended amount is based on the child's age, gender, etc. It can be hard to find the right number, but the American Heart Association should be a good start. Check their website.

Family Meals

It is shown that three family meals a week leads to healthier kids, according to a study. It is proven that children's eating habit in the early stage of their development often lasts forever. The study showed that the family decreased their unhealthy food intake by about a fifth of their usual intake, which is a very big deal considering the obesity epidemic today.

Water

Of course, when one speaks about dieting and meals, very few consider what to drink. After all, there are way fewer choices compared to eating options. A study in the American Journal of Public Health shows that many children, especially in America, do not drink enough water. Most of the time, they drink something else instead which is a lot less healthy. Things like soda should not be drunk and replace water. Because they are sweet and energetic with that delicious touch of fizz, it can be hard for parents to stop their children from drinking sugary drinks. The children cannot be blamed, either. Those drinks are addictive, and it can be hard to stop once anyone starts to drink it regularly. So, here are a few tips to convince children to stop drinking sugary drinks and start drinking water instead.

Start by teaching them the importance of drinking water, for their health and development. Humans have survived this far not because they drink soda, but water. Another method is leading by example. Parents often have a hard time teaching their children to drink water when they themselves don't drink water.

Moreover, always have a bottle of water handy and drink from it instead of buying a can of soda. Better yet, freeze some water so children can freshen up quickly after they have a tiring play session. This works best during summer. Stay hydrated.

When out eating or going anywhere, parents should also encourage their children to choose water instead of other sugary beverages. If the children complain that plain water is too... plain, try adding slices of berries, lime or lemon to give it a taste and make it fun.

Chapter 5: Increasing Appetite

Children should both eat more and eat properly. In the previous chapter, the ways children can start to eat healthy food have been discussed. This chapter looks at how children's appetite can be increased. It can be tricky, but not impossible. There are ways to make them eat more and eat better.

Breakfast

Having a good, healthy breakfast is needed to increase a child's appetite. A balanced breakfast will help the body consume food and produce energy better for the rest of the day. Many people, including children, feel hungry after about 4 to 5 hours. So, after sleeping for about 8-10 hours, everyone will feel quite hungry in the morning. Having breakfast then will give children the energy they need for the rest of the day.

Water

While on the topic of mornings, children should also drink water every morning. In fact, they should do it the first thing in the morning. Just like food, people need to drink water often, a lot more often than eating. So, sleeping for several hours without drinking any water, and everyone will wake up feeling very thirsty. The same can also be said for children. They should drink water first thing in the morning, even before they have their milk. Drinking water about thirty minutes before a meal helps the body a lot.

Snacks

To have a better appetite, try considering eating snacks as meals instead. No, not in the form of eating multiple tubes of Pringles. Rather, instead of eating Pringles, eat a sandwich. Instead of French fries, have muesli or cereal. Instead of eating unhealthy snacks, eat healthy ones.

Nuts

Nuts are considered to be one of the best snacks out there. They are relatively healthy, and have protein-building properties, not to mention that they also help boost a child's appetite. Either eat nut butters or roast nuts.

Milk

Many children who have a hard time eating a lot, often drink too much milk. Basically, when children drink milk as fillers, appetizers, or simply as snacks, they will no longer feel as hungry. Try out other dairy products instead such as cottage cheese, yogurt, or cream.

Favorite Food

Everyone has that one food they know they can stand eating every day, in large amounts. For some children who have a low appetite, the sight of food alone can cause problems. However, when the same child sees that their parents are cooking his or her favorite food, they are more willing to eat. When the child's appetite has increased, then healthy (or healthier) food can be introduced into their meals.

Small Bites

A way to improve a child's appetite is by teaching them to eat small bites of food at a time. Smaller bites over time will increase their appetite, allowing them to eat more and more. Then, they will start eating on their own and decide on the bite-size themselves.

Yogurt

Yogurt is very important for a child. It is a dairy product that has substances to improve the child's appetite as well as the immune system, which protect them from becoming sick. Plus, yogurt is great for dessert as well.

Pungent or Strong Food

Sometimes, a child's appetite can be affected by extreme odors or overpowering tastes. If the child has a low appetite, check the kitchen if there are food odors or if the food itself has a strong taste of garlic, and so on. Removing these and the child's appetite should start working again.

Spices

Okay, hold on. It is true that too strong a taste can ruin a child's appetite. Still, that's no excuse to cook a child's meal bland. Add some spices to... spice things up. Oregano, coriander, fennel, or cinnamon are all good spices and herbs that help to build an appetite. Add a small amount here and there, and the child should start eating more.

Oily Food

Avoid oily food like the plague. They kill children's appetite. Some families enjoy eating this oily food, often from fast foods in the U.S. Go easy on those fatty products and dairy because these might be the reason why the child has a low appetite.

Exercise

It should go without saying that playing sports or simply exercising improves appetite in both adults and children. Sometimes, it is because of the fact that they have too much energy in them, and their body does not need to take in extra energy from food. So, the best way is to drain all of that energy by playing or exercising. It will increase appetite while making the body and mind stronger as well. Talk about hitting two birds with one stone.

Warmth

Sometimes, a child's appetite may decrease if it is too hot or stuffy inside. This is fair. Who would want to eat dinner when it feels like they are in an oven? So, opening the window and sitting the child close to it helps freshen up their eating time a bit. If it is already cool and fresh inside, perhaps the problem lies with the fact that the child sits too low at the table. Consider getting a high chair and their appetite might be increased.

Fresh Lime Juice

A child may fuss over food and say that they are not hungry. In that case, try letting them drink sweetened fresh lime juice instead of water. Lime helps their body digest food better and increase their appetite as well.

Another way to improve a child's appetite is by giving them ginger juice with honey and peppermint chutneys. These can be made at home very easily and improve their immune system as well.

Table Topics

It is normal and even encouraged, to have family meals. Sometimes, parents discuss how should they spend their money or plan for the child's school schedule when the family eats together. Still, serious or stressful topics should be avoided at all costs. The stress and feelings for both adults and child will turn bad, and it will ruin both the appetite of adults and children alike. So, try to talk about happy things instead.

Zinc

Zinc is very useful in building an appetite. They can be found in pumpkin seeds, wheat, and cashew nuts. Having a good level of zinc in the body will improve the child's appetite, so try to have a child eat that food during meals or snacks. Another easy way to do it is by using zinc supplements.

Chapter 6: Socialization

Children have many problems the moment they are born into this world. All adults have been through the same thing. One of the biggest problems is socializing. Being able to develop social skills and interact with the world around them is crucial to children's development. This is even more important than being able to get a good grade in the classroom. However, there are many skills to be learned, such as talking effectively, talking to strangers, starting a conversation, listening, getting along with people, the list goes on. It is important to point out that some kids are better at socializing than others. They can deal with being teased, bullied, awkwardness, and popularity properly. Some others are not so fortunate. However, there are ways that children can hone their social skill. Here are a few ways to improve:

Eye-Contact

Children should learn how to look into people's eyes when they talk to them. This builds confidence and makes communication feel smooth and honest. This can be easily done by playing the "Staring Contest" game or talking to toys. There is another trick to this. Instead of staring into people's eyes, children can also look at the forehead, brows, or between the eyes of whoever they are talking to. The other person cannot tell anyway.

Communicate

This is rather obvious, but children should learn how to interact, respond, or express their opinions or what they think by speaking or by gestures. Knowing the appropriate greetings and response are good starting points for children. They also need to learn how to stop being shy, and a good way is to make sure they understand that it is okay for them to speak their mind and that not doing so would only make the situation worse for everyone. Plus, a good way of overcoming shyness is to think of the worst possible scenario. Even if they did something poorly, it is not the end of the world for them, and people will forget about it eventually. So, there is really no reason to be shy.

So, children should know how to talk, ask questions, and express with honesty their needs, what they want, what they believe in. They should also get into a habit of saying "Please," "Thank you," etc.

Environment

A lonely child will have a problem in interacting in the world. They need good company, exposure, as well as the chances to start talking to their friends or classmates. They will talk to different people, and that is the best-case scenario because they will experience different types of people and understand how to talk to those people and fit in properly.

The best way is to let them talk to other children and play around. This is the best socialization practice they will get at an early age. Sometimes, children who cannot socialize properly will have troubles understanding other people's feelings based on their face. To counter this problem, children should get into activities that get them more comfortable. Just like adults, the best way to socialize outside of school is by going to other events. That is why it is important for children to get into a hobby so that they can talk to other children who have a similar interest. Otherwise, children who are into sports also have plenty of friends to make in their own team. All of this talking will develop a child's social skills and help them develop their own personality and become a unique person.

Chapter 7: Emotional Control

Both adults and children have a hard time controlling their emotions. Sometimes, parents have a hard time getting their children to speak their mind. In other cases, parents don't really listen, and so children often feel left out. Therefore, the best course of action is for both parents and children to take some time off so parents can teach their children how to manage their feelings. This also benefits the young one as they too can tell their parents what they feel, and perhaps the family will be more bearable for both sides.

Let's face it, a family is not really what people say. Jordan Peterson said that a family is like a group of people standing in a circle with their hands at each other neck, squeezing just hard enough to strangle one another in twenty years. Is that bad? Yes. Can the situation be better? Absolutely. It is possible for a family to be a loving group of people looking out for each other like people say, but it can take some time.

It all starts with children learning how to control their emotions. There are many benefits that children could get from being able to control their emotions. One of which is the ability to pay better attention, or being able to properly interact with other people, not to mention that children can control their own impulses. By no means does emotional control mean that children need to suppress their emotion and not talk about it. That is a very bad idea, and could literally ruin the development of a child.

Think of emotional control as a way for children to say what they want without annoying the adults. Why is this a good idea? Well, adults, and anyone really, is more willing to give children and other people what they want if they are polite about it. Screaming and kicking is not going to work very well, especially in public. Parents will be embarrassed, people will dislike the children, and the children will sometimes get what they want, sometimes they don't and get punished for it. Children who can control their own emotions will do better while socializing as well.

So, really, everyone can win if both children and parents can talk to each other clearly. Both give up one thing, but overall everyone gets something. The child may promise not to yell or throw a tantrum if the parents buy them something that they want, or if they can't for a good reason they will give something else in return, and the child should just accept it. That sounds like a great system for both children and their parents. So, how can such a system be created?

Be Open

First, it is important for children to understand what they can feel and why. This is important because if the child does not know what they want or understand why they feel that way, it is hard for both parents and children to figure out what is wrong. Adults don't suddenly burst into tears, and children are the same. Sometimes, it is just that they don't know how to say why they are feeling that way. This could lead to the children throwing tantrums. Set aside some time so parents can tell their children more about their own feelings and why they feel and behave that way. So, next time when something goes wrong, the kids can tell their parents about their feelings. Even if they can't, the parents should be able to tell what is wrong and fix the problem. Communication is key.

Understanding

At the same time, children should also understand how others are feeling just by looking at how people react. Here, parents should be responsible for teaching their children about how to read people's reactions. That way, at least children know how to behave in any situation based on the people around them. This also helps them build more meaningful and beneficial relationships.

How to Cope

Children should have a way to control their own emotions. Again, parents should help them in finding which method is the best. There is one thing that children should know: "It's okay," It's okay to lose control sometimes. It is okay to feel upset. It is okay to feel jealous. It is okay to be angry. Those are very normal even among adults, but feeling emotions and letting them out are two different things. Feeling something cannot be avoided, but taking it out can be controlled.

There should be a way for children to cope with their emotions. Since every child is different, they will need different techniques to calm down as well. Here are some suggestions: listen to music, draw, color, go to a quiet place, squeeze a stress ball or stuffed animal (hard), blow bubbles, drink some cold water, etc. It depends, so both parents and children need to work a bit and find out what works.

Write

Sometimes, writing stories help children understand how to control their emotions. When things that cause children to lose control are found as well as the way to cope with those problems, it is time to sit down and write a short story. This serves as a way for children to think of the time when they will face those things and understand how they should react so there won't be a disaster. It is important for children to practice imagining such a situation so they can practice how to cope with the problem.

Practice

This can be done by both parents and children, although it should be clear that it should be done by parents. When the child doesn't use their coping method to calm down and regain control, parents should give feedback.

It is important to do so only after the child is calm. If the feedback is given while they are upset, it will only make them more upset. When children are calm again, they can think more clearly and will be able to understand that there could be a better way to handle the situation.

For children, however, things are a bit tricky. They need to first understand that they can handle any problem without freaking out and screaming. Then, they also need to understand that they should practice performing their coping method every day to form a coping habit. With this habit created, children should be able to use their coping method regularly whenever they need to calm down.

Practicing can also be done by role-playing. It can be upsetting for children, but doing this helps children cope when the real problem occurs. Parents should work with their children through different upsetting situations. Through practice and discussion of every upsetting thing that could happen to children, they are better prepared for future events. One way to know if role-playing works is by letting the child say how would they react to a certain situation and then parents should give some more advice.

Chapter 8: Other Habits

In addition to the previous pointers, there are a few habits that children should pick up as well so they can become a role model and a better person in the future.

Clean Up

Children should at least learn how to clean up their own room. Although it is just one room, it teaches them a lot. Children will be able to see what is the problem in their own room and set it right. Plus, neither children nor adults want to walk into a messy room. Here is a tip: Start by making the bed. Everything else will seem easier.

Money

Children should also learn how to spend their money responsibly when they are old enough to start spending money. A good way to do it is by getting them into a habit of saving money. Another way to do it is by rewarding them with a small amount of money whenever they finish a chore. This ties in perfectly with the cleaning up habit, among many other habits.

Children will then understand the value of money.

Honest

Honesty is important. Children should tell the truth, or at least don't lie (because sometimes the truth is unknown). It is true that telling the truth can and will lead to trouble, but it is better to run into trouble than not being trusted.

Hygiene

Hygiene is important for children's health. Washing hands after touching dirty things, showering and brushing teeth at least twice a day, keeping the hair clean, the nails short, are a few habits that children should have. This helps them in several ways. As stated earlier, their immune system will be stronger, and they will not fall ill as often. Another benefit is that they are more attractive to other kids. Again, just like adults, no one wants to talk to someone who has smelly breath. Children who are clean have a higher chance of making friends.

Helping Others

Having a helpful nature is also important. Being humble and generous means that children will grow into a respectable and lovable person in the future. So, parents should teach their child to lend a helping hand to other people whenever possible. Still, just be careful around strangers.

No Smoking, Drinking, and Drugs

Habits such as smoking, drinking, and drugs depend on the background of the family and what comes afterward. It should be clear that smoking, drinking, and doing drugs are bad, no matter how "cool" it may look. It will only ruin the future. Here, children need to understand peer pressure, which is when all of a child's friends are doing one thing and that the child feels that he or she should do the same thing as well. Most of the time, such pressure should be resisted. However, should a child remain disciplined and resist the urge, they will need support from their parents.

Chapter 9: Conclusion

This is the end of the book. Hopefully, this book has some useful pointers that both parents and children are able to practice to aid in the child's development. To sum it all up, there are only a few things that both children and their parents should understand.

For parents, try to understand a child's impulses. They are young and vulnerable, after all. They are only impulsive and throw a tantrum because those that they depend on the most, the parents, sometimes don't do things that they hope their parents would do for them. It is up to the parents to teach their children so they would understand how the world works.

Treat children with kindness and understanding. Most importantly, listen to what they have to say. They may say a few bad things, but there are always some messages that show how they truly feel. Don't turn down their opinion only because they are young and don't understand a thing about the world. They can be right sometimes, too. And, when there is an argument, know that the goal is to solve the problem, not to win. Winning an argument against a child would only make them feel disconnected and unloved.

Children should also give their parents some break. Parents have a lot of things to do to raise a single child. That nine-month period before birth was already dreadful for the mother. If anything, the one thing parents wish their children would do is understand. To do this, communication is key. This applies to both sides, in fact. Talking openly about how one feels is the best way to improve almost any situation. Also, children should also learn how to compromise and trust that, sometimes, parents know best.

Printed in Great Britain
by Amazon